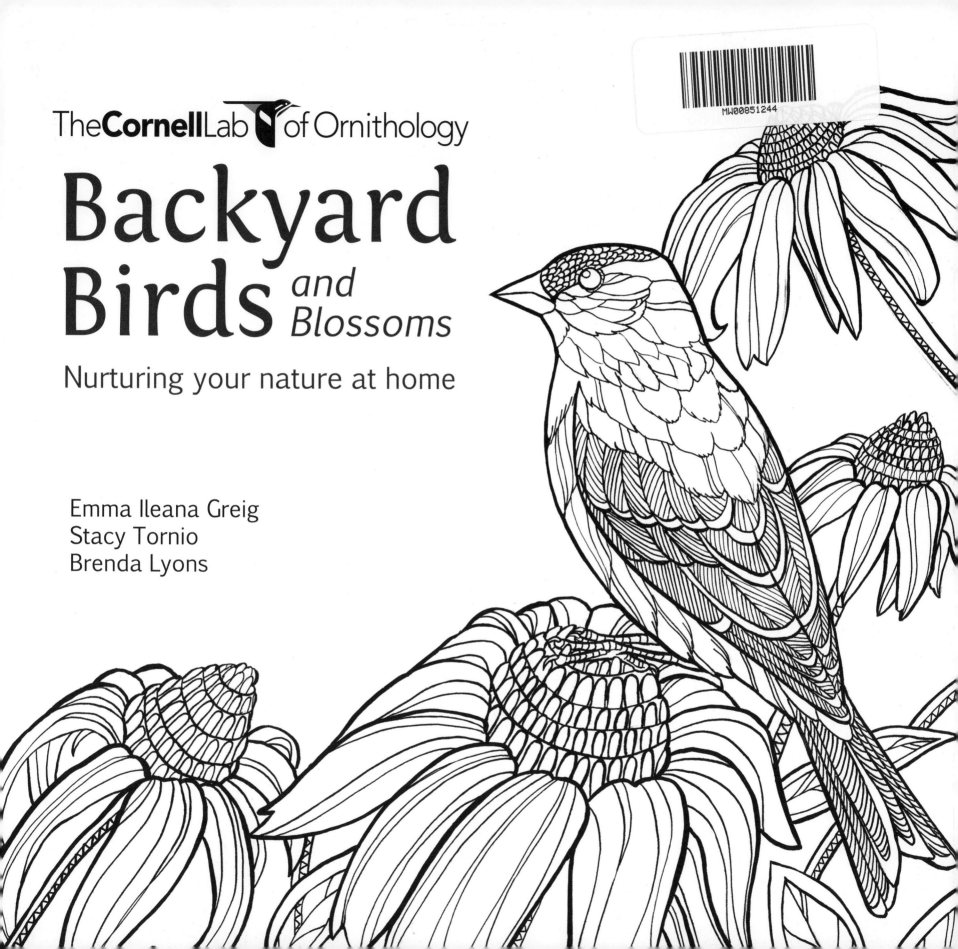

The Cornell Lab of Ornithology

Backyard Birds *and Blossoms*

Nurturing your nature at home

Emma Ileana Greig
Stacy Tornio
Brenda Lyons

Text by Emma Ileana Greig & Stacy Tornio

Design by Patricia Mitter

ISBN: 978-1-943645-24-4

Printed in China

Library of Congress Cataloging-in-Publication Data available.

10 9 8 7 6 5 4 3 2 1

Produced by the

Cornell Lab Publishing Group

120A North Salem Street

Apex, NC 27502

www.CornellLabpg.com

MIX
Paper from
responsible sources
FSC® C124385

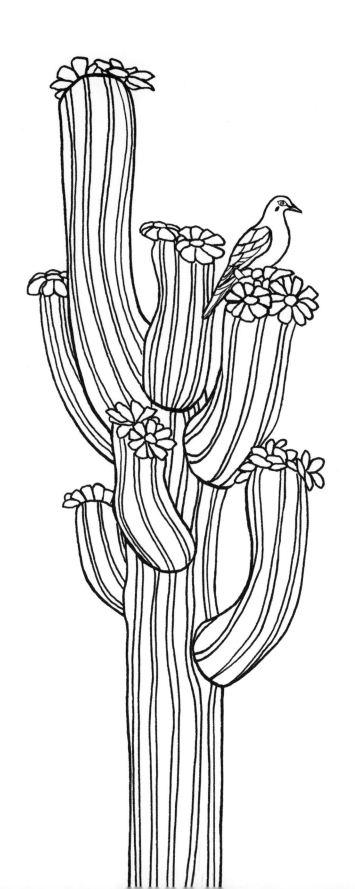

INTRODUCTION

You may think of nature as something remote or pristine, but it's all around you to explore, especially where you live. *Backyard Birds and Blossoms* celebrates the rich diversity of life that you can find right outside your own doorsteps.

Whether urban, suburban or rural, you can find birds and plants inhabiting the outdoor spaces that surround your home. *Backyard Birds and Blossoms* is filled with breathtaking coloring scenes that demonstrate how people in different places nurture birds and wildlife in their yards. From an urban rooftop garden rich with sparrows and swifts, to a natural pond filled with tadpoles and dragonflies, you will see that there are many ways to bring wildlife to your yard, no matter where you live.

Throughout the coloring pages inside, we've paired birds with native blossoms, bird feeders, nest boxes, and other elements that attract and support backyard birds, to create unique and stunning backyard landscapes for you to color. Along the way, you'll discover some amazing things about birds and their behaviors, such as how California Scrub-Jays bury peanuts instead of eating them. You'll also learn about plants that can attract new birds to your yard, such as tiny Verdins that will drink from bright pink cactus blossoms, even in the hottest climates.

Enjoy these fun snippets of biology as you color the fantastic petals and plumes in the pages that follow.

At the back of *Backyard Birds and Blossoms*, you will also find a guide to bird feeders and food from the Cornell Lab, which will help you learn the art of bird feeding and how to attract all sorts of different species.

And, if you like to feed birds, you can turn this pastime into so much more by participating in an exciting citizen-science program from the Cornell Lab of Ornithology and Bird Studies Canada, called Project FeederWatch. By identifying and counting your feeder birds and sending your counts to Project FeederWatch, you can contribute to a 30-year and growing data set that informs us all about how our backyard birds are faring. Over 50 million people in North America feed birds each year, but only 20,000 participate in Project FeederWatch. You can make a difference by participating and becoming a biologist in your own backyard.

We hope that you enjoy using your imagination to color the beautiful pages of *Backyard Birds and Blossoms*, and that you are inspired to put that imagination to work at home by creating a haven for birds and other wildlife in your own backyard!

— Emma Ileana Greig, Author

BIRD QR COMPANION APP

To enrich your coloring experience, we've created a special app that you can use with this book—Bird QR—a dedicated book companion app that helps to bring to life this and other books, free from the Cornell Lab Publishing Group.

Bird QR lets you listen to bird songs and calls from species throughout this book, and also access more detailed information on each bird in this book from the Cornell Lab's #1 birding website, *AllAboutBirds.org*.

To download Bird QR, simply visit the Apple or Android store and search "Bird QR" to download. Once downloaded, open the app and touch "Tap To Start," which will bring you to the main menu screen. From there, you can begin scanning symbols in the book by touching the "Scan Book QR Now" button, or navigate to other app screens. Look for and scan these symbols throughout *Backyard Birds and Blossoms* pages:

 Listen to Bird Sounds. Each bird species page in this book has this symbol to listen to bird sounds on that page with Bird QR. Simply scan the symbol and choose the sounds you want to hear.

 Open Website URL. When you see this symbol on a page in this book and scan with Bird QR, it will open your browser and take you to a specific web page to learn more.

Look for new capabilities and functions of the Bird QR app such as video streaming in future updates. Please enjoy this app and visit *CornellLabPG.com* to learn more about other books from the Cornell Lab Publishing Group.

— Brian Scott Sockin, Publisher

LEARN MORE ABOUT BIRDS

The Cornell Lab of Ornithology is a nonprofit organization dedicated to improving the understanding and protection of birds. Our hallmarks are scientific excellence and technological innovation to advance the understanding of nature, and to engage people of all ages in learning about birds and protecting the planet. Beyond the pages of this book, we hope you'll enjoy these 10 ways to keep learning more about birds.

1. Identify birds with the Merlin Bird ID app.
It's exciting to see a new bird, especially when you can clinch the identification! For help, download the free Merlin Bird ID app. Merlin will ask you five questions to help you identify the birds around you. To get Merlin, visit the Apple or Android store and type in "Merlin," OR type *bit.ly/downloadmerlin*, OR scan this symbol with your Bird QR companion app.

2. Delve into a wealth of information using All About Birds.
Learn more about your favorite birds on the All About Birds website. Explore fascinating facts, sounds, photos, range maps, and more. Visit *AllAboutBirds.org* in your browser or scan this symbol with your Bird QR companion app.

3. Take your understanding to the next level with the Cornell Lab Bird Academy.
Try fun online activities that teach you about bird biology, including behavior and anatomy. You can also sign up for courses ranging from bird identification webinars to the college-level course, *Ornithology: Comprehensive Bird Biology*. Visit *Academy.AllAboutBirds.org* in your browser or scan this symbol with your Bird QR companion app.

4. Enjoy live, close-up views with Bird Cams.
Watch as hawks, owls, and other birds raise their young. See colorful birds at locations across the country, featured on our feeder cams. Visit *Cams.AllAboutBirds.org* in your browser or scan this symbol with your Bird QR companion app.

5. Watch birds and share what you see with a citizen-science project.
By recording your observations, you can contribute to science and conservation. The Cornell Lab invites you to participate in the Great Backyard Bird Count, Project FeederWatch, eBird, NestWatch, Celebrate Urban Birds, and Habitat Network. Visit *Birds.Cornell.edu* or scan this symbol with your Bird QR companion app.

6. Explore the world's birds with the Macaulay Library.
Hear the sounds of wildlife from around the world or watch their behaviors in videos. Search for a bird you have in mind or browse hundreds of thousands of recordings. Visit *MacaulayLibrary.org* or scan this symbol with your Bird QR companion app.

7. Share BirdSleuth with a child or a teacher.
The BirdSleuth K–12 curriculum engages kids in scientific inquiry and learning about birds outdoors. You can get your school interested in birds or enjoy the activities with kids at home. Visit *BirdSleuth.org* or scan this symbol with your Bird QR companion app.

8. Join the Cornell Lab's Facebook community.
Connect with others who love birds, and get your daily dose of bird quizzes, photos, and fun facts about birds. Visit *Facebook.com/Cornellbirds* or scan this symbol with your Bird QR companion app.

9. Learn more about the fascinating lives of birds in
Living Bird **magazine.**

Enjoy spectacular photographs of birds and gain new insights from in-depth articles. This quarterly magazine comes right to your mailbox when you join as a member of the Cornell Lab. Your support gives back to the birds by advancing the Lab's conservation mission. Visit *Birds.Cornell.edu/Join* or scan this symbol with your Bird QR companion app.

10. Discover more about birds every month with
Cornell Lab eNews.

It's easy to keep in touch with the latest news and ideas about birds. This free newsletter brings the beauty of birds right to your email box. Visit *Birds.Cornell.edu/eNews* or scan this symbol with your Bird QR companion app.

ACKNOWLEDGMENTS

Thanks to the participants of Project FeederWatch for their dedication to science and nature in their own backyards—they helped discover many of the bird population trends that inspired the pages of this book. Thanks to the photographers who donated photos for the book, many of whom were participants in Project FeederWatch and the Great Backyard Bird Count. Thanks to Anne Marie Johnson, Chelsea Benson, and Kerrie Wilcox for their tireless efforts running Project FeederWatch at the Cornell Lab of Ornithology and Bird Studies Canada. Thanks to Kevin McGowan for offering his meticulous critiques of bird form and concepts. Thanks to Mary Guthrie, Diane Tessaglia-Hymes, and Patricia Mitter for their efforts and insights throughout the creation of this book. Special thanks to Miyoko Chu for providing an exceptional balance of guidance and creativity, and to Brian Scott Sockin for providing endless enthusiasm and inspiration. And finally, thanks to our families and friends: Diane, Richard, Lily Greig, Talia Chinn, Fran Rogers, and Francis D'Agostine.

"In memory of David Lyons, who encouraged my love of books and art from the very beginning."
— *Brenda L.*

NORTHERN CARDINALS
and crabapple

Have you seen a male cardinal "kissing" his mate? He is offering her food—a gift to demonstrate his value as a partner and provider. Northern Cardinals love sunflower and safflower seeds, and appreciate large feeders, such as hopper feeders, to perch comfortably while they eat.

BLOSSOM: Crabapples have appeal year-round, from the beautiful blooms in spring to the small fruit the trees produce in late summer or early fall. If you're planting a crabapple to attract birds, look for a variety with smaller fruit.

Northern Cardinal

Northern
Cardinals

COOPER'S HAWK
and redbud tree

By landscaping your yard with plants that attract songbirds and other wildlife, you might also attract hawks. It's always thrilling to see a hawk flying overhead or even perched in your yard. Some, such as Cooper's Hawks, will hunt other birds. If you place feeders near bushes or branches, small birds can survey the feeders before alighting on them, or dive for refuge if a hawk suddenly arrives.

BLOSSOM: Redbud trees are some of the very first to bloom in the spring. This makes their blooms really stand out because most haven't even leafed out yet. This gorgeous tree is common in the East, fairly easy to grow, and gets up to 30 feet tall.

Cooper's Hawk

Cooper's Hawk

RUBY-THROATED HUMMINGBIRDS
and columbine

One of the first signs of spring is the arrival of hummingbirds, ruby-throated in the East and black-chinned in the West. Hummingbirds learn from experience that red flowers tend to be excellent food sources, which is why they are attracted to red nectar feeders. Planting red, nectar-producing flowers will also bring hummingbirds to your yard, and will save you the trouble of refilling the sugar water!

BLOSSOM: Columbine is one of the easiest native flowers you can grow in your backyard. It doesn't grow tall (usually only a foot), but the flowers are a rich source of nectar for hummingbirds, butterflies, and other insects.

Ruby-throated Hummingbird

Ruby-throated
Hummingbirds

CHESTNUT-BACKED CHICKADEE
and coral bells

Many birds will appreciate your offer of nesting material. Provide short fluffy strands such as pet hair in a wire cage and watch birds build their nests in spring. Even species such as Chestnut-backed Chickadees may pay you a visit for some nest lining. Chestnut-backed Chickadees live in the Pacific Northwest and sport rich brown plumage on their flanks and back, quite distinct from their more widespread Black-capped and Carolina chickadee relatives.

BLOSSOM: Coral bells (*Heuchera*) might be known for their gorgeous foliage colors of burgundy, orange, and even hues of blue, but this plant offers so much more. It blooms a lot earlier than many summer plants, making it a great nectar stopover for butterflies and hummingbirds. The flowers are small, but hummingbirds love them.

Chestnut-backed Chickadee

Chestnut-backed
Chickadee

ROSE-BREASTED GROSBEAKS
and trumpet honeysuckle

With a bright red splash of color on their chest, male Rose-breasted Grosbeaks help their mates at the nest. Grosbeaks eat fruit, seeds, and bugs when they arrive in the spring. When incubating their eggs, females will sing. In late summer, most Rose-breasted Grosbeaks migrate, but Project FeederWatch participants have reported occasional "stragglers" in northern states stopping in for a snack in the cold winter months.

BLOSSOM: Honeysuckle sometimes has the reputation of being invasive, but not the native species! Look for the botanical name *Lonicera sempervirens*. This plant with beautiful coral blooms can grow up to 15 feet and 6 feet wide. It's perfect for a trellis or arbor.

Rose-breasted Grosbeak

Rose-breasted
Grosbeaks

EASTERN BLUEBIRDS
and viburnum

In spring, attract bluebirds to your yard with nest boxes. Eastern Bluebirds will often raise two broods in a season, and pairs will team up to accomplish this task. While the female is crafting the second nest and laying the second clutch of eggs, the male will care for the fledged young from the first nest. Now that's teamwork!

BLOSSOM: Viburnum is truly a plant with four-season appeal. It has flowers in the spring, great foliage through summer and fall, and then berries in fall and winter. It's one of the most bird-friendly shrubs you can purchase, and there are more than 150 varieties from which to choose! Ask a local garden expert or native plant society for their recommendation on what's best for your area.

Eastern Bluebird

Eastern Bluebirds

AMERICAN GOLDFINCHES
and coneflowers

The sunny yellow plumage of American Goldfinches brightens up any backyard. Did you know that those bright yellow feathers disappear in winter, replaced with more subtle grayish-yellow plumes in spring? Goldfinches only need their bright plumage when they are trying to attract a mate in the spring and summer. In fall, they molt into a duller garb, which is safer because it attracts less attention from predators.

BLOSSOM: It's very common to see a finch perched on a coneflower, digging out its seeds. Look for native purple coneflowers at a local plant sale (*Echinacea* will be in the name). These are great for providing seeds to birds, and then they'll often multiply on their own.

American Goldfinch

American Goldfinches

WHITE-WINGED DOVES
and saguaro

White-winged Doves love hot pink saguaro fruit and white saguaro flowers, and they also love backyards. Counts from Project FeederWatch show us that White-winged Doves are expanding their range dramatically in southern states. Enjoy any species of dove in your backyard by offering seeds on a platform feeder, which they will visit with enthusiasm.

BLOSSOM: If you ever get the chance to see a saguaro cactus blooming, definitely stop and take pictures! The blooms last for less than 24 hours, just enough time for bees, birds, butterflies, and bats to pollinate them.

White-winged Dove

White-winged Doves

PAINTED BUNTINGS
and coreopsis

Painted Buntings may be one of the most colorful birds in North America, with stunning red, green, and purple plumage. They will visit feeders for millet in late summer, when they have finished feeding their young. To attract them to your yard all spring and summer, offer a birdbath. They might not be able to resist a quick splash!

BLOSSOM: Also called tickseed, coreopsis thrives in full sun and is drought-tolerant. This is a great native plant to add to your collection because it's also popular among butterflies and bees. Some gardeners even swear that it's resistant to deer.

Painted Bunting

Painted Buntings

SONG SPARROWS
AND HOUSE FINCHES
with zinnias

Your vegetable garden may offer a meal for more than just you. Gardens are havens for sparrows and finches to find seeds and insects. Song Sparrows, with their vivid springtime song and dark spot on the chest, are familiar yard visitors. House Finches, with their red, orange, or yellow hues, may enjoy foraging in your garden as well.

BLOSSOM: Zinnias are one of the easiest flowers to grow from seed in the spring. You just sow the seeds directly into the ground, and then they'll bring you color for months. They'll also bring you bees and butterflies. You can find a lot of new zinnia varieties on the market today, so don't be afraid to go outside of the norm with this flower.

Song Sparrow   House Finch

Song Sparrows and House Finches

BALTIMORE ORIOLES
and dogwood

A flute-like song from the treetops in spring reveals the arrival of Baltimore Orioles. Males defend territories on which females build pendulous nests, carefully woven with grasses and fibers. To get a close look at these treetop dwellers, offer fruit such as oranges stuck on a spike or a small dish of fruit jelly.

BLOSSOM: The berries from dogwood trees are some of the best for birds. They have a very high fat content, making them perfect fuel for migrating birds in the fall. You can find several native dogwood trees and shrubs in your area, so check with a local horticulturalist or arborist for specific recommendations.

Baltimore Oriole

Baltimore Orioles

GAMBEL'S QUAIL AND CACTUS WREN
with cholla

It is hard to get much cuter than chunky Gambel's Quail, with their soft clucking calls and their perky topknot. Families of quail tend to stick together, investigating the ground for seeds and roosting together in low vegetation. Attract them to your yard by providing millet or a shallow tray of water on the ground, and enjoy watching them forage as a family.

BLOSSOM: Even if you live in a dry or desert climate, you can still have plenty of life and color in your garden. Look for cholla and yucca plants for your area. There are several options out there with beautiful flowers, and your local garden center should be able to point you in the right direction.

Gambel's Quail

Cactus Wren

Gambel's Quail and Cactus Wren

MOURNING DOVE
and petunias

The soothing *co-OO-oo* of the Mourning Dove gives it its mournful name. Data from Project FeederWatch confirm that they are one of the most common feeder visitors in North America, although you wouldn't think they could reproduce with the flimsy nests that they build! Perhaps that is why nest placement is so important for Mourning Doves, such as in a nice planter of petunias in your backyard (but water with care!).

BLOSSOM: Need a flower for a hanging basket that will stay bright and colorful all season? This is it! Gardeners love petunias because they last for months, and they are a reliable source of nectar in spring, summer, and fall. Plus, if you're lucky, you just might get a bird such as a Mourning Dove or wren to nest in your hanging basket.

Mourning Dove

Mourning Dove

YELLOW WARBLERS
and flowering dogwood

Sweet sweet sweet I'm so sweet sings the male Yellow Warbler in spring. Yellow Warblers nest all across North America, and they fine-tune their nest construction to match the climate. In colder northern locations, their nests are thick and warm. In warmer southern locations, the nests are thinner, which makes them easier to construct. What clever little birds warblers are!

BLOSSOM: When it comes to dogwood trees, you can find quite the variety for backyards. The flowering dogwood (*Cornus florida*) is probably one of the most popular, followed by the similar Japanese flowering dogwood (*Cornus kousa*). For those living in the West, try Pacific dogwood (*Cornus nuttallii*).

Yellow Warbler

Yellow Warblers

VIOLET-GREEN SWALLOWS
and butterfly weed

The glossy feathers of Violet-green Swallows are heart-stoppingly beautiful when seen in a beam of sunlight. Watch these masters of flight in your backyard by nurturing unmowed areas, which will attract aerial insects, and by extension, insect-eating birds such as swallows.

BLOSSOM: A lot of people don't realize butterfly weed is part of the milkweed family, but it is. This perennial does well in full sun and has small (but gorgeous) yellow and orange blooms. As you might guess by its name, butterflies adore it.

Violet-green Swallow

Violet-green Swallows

GREAT BLUE HERON
and water lilies

Having a small pond in your backyard can attract a special suite of water-loving visitors, such as herons, frogs, and dragonflies. The Great Blue Heron is the largest heron species in North America. Although they prefer fish, they will feast on almost anything they can catch, including amphibians, reptiles, and occasionally, small mammals.

BLOSSOM: You might not think of water lilies as a good nectar plant, but they can be! Think of how many insects are naturally drawn to water, and they need plants and flowers to pollinate. They will definitely add color to your backyard pond, while supporting bees and other pollinators.

Great Blue Heron

Great Blue Heron

SUMMER TANAGER
and black-eyed Susans

The theme of the Summer Tanager is red! Adult males are completely red, while young males show a beautiful dappling of both red and green plumage. If you are lucky enough to have one in your backyard, you may notice it feeding on wasps or bees. Some Project FeederWatch participants have even observed Summer Tanagers nibbling on suet in colder months.

BLOSSOM: Black-eyed Susans are some of the most reliable perennials you can grow in your backyard. They are easy to find, there are several options to choose from, they are drought-tolerant, and the birds love the seeds. When finding a black-eyed Susan for your garden, look for the botanical name. Common native varieties include *Rudbeckia hirta* and *Rudbeckia fulgida*.

Summer Tanager

SUMMER
TANAGER

VERDINS AND PYRRHULOXIA
with yucca

In hot, arid environments, a shallow birdbath can be the best thing you can offer your feathered friends. Pyrrhuloxias, desert-dwelling relatives of the Northern Cardinal, will appreciate the drink. Nurture plants that offer natural sources of liquid, such as the nectar in ocotillo blossoms, which cute yellow-headed Verdins will drink with enthusiasm!

BLOSSOM: Yucca is proof that you can combine the striking foliage of succulents along with the beautiful blooms of perennials. It sends up tall stems with white flowers in the middle of its spiky base, and is one of the most drought-tolerant perennials you can add to your garden. It will look good for years.

Verdin   Pyrrhuloxia

Verdins and Pyrrhuloxia

INDIGO BUNTING
with asters and goldenrod

You won't find a more strikingly blue bird than a male Indigo Bunting. Listen for its song in spring, a series of double notes coming from a sunny field. Young males learn their songs from older neighbors. You might be fortunate enough to see buntings up close at your feeders by offering fruits and small seeds.

BLOSSOM: Chances are, you've seen goldenrod growing in the wild, along the roadside or in meadows. This native wildflower also has a great place in your home garden. It's drought-tolerant and lasts well into the fall. Plant in groups to create a swathe of gold. You can also pair it with perennials such as asters, which typically have bright pink and purple shades, to really create an impact in the garden.

Indigo Bunting

BLACK-CHINNED HUMMINGBIRDS
and bee balm

In the heat of summer, offering a small fountain can provide a delightful source of water for hummingbirds. Hummingbirds typically beat their wings more than 50 times a second, which can work up quite a bit of heat. They will splash in the sprinkles and appreciate the cooling effect.

BLOSSOM: If you want to attract bees, then bee balm is one of the best flowers you can grow. As a bonus, it's also one of the best plants for hummingbirds, especially since these tiny jeweled fliers are so strongly attracted to red. Look for the botanical name, *Monarda*, for native varieties in your area.

Black-chinned Hummingbird

Black-chinned
Hummingbirds

SPOTTED TOWHEE
and milkweed

If you hear rustling in the leaves and see bits of debris flying left and right, you might be in the presence of a towhee. Towhees love to forage on the ground, using a two-footed backwards hop to kick leaves out of their way, revealing delicious morsels of insects and seeds. The rufous patches on their sides and their bright red eyes will help you identify them.

BLOSSOM: You can find many varieties of milkweed on the market today, but the common milkweed (*Asclepias syriaca*) is the most widespread. You can often find this one growing in the wild, but it's also an excellent choice for backyards. It usually grows up to 5 feet, and it has bright pink blooms in the peak of summer.

Spotted Towhee

Spotted Towhee

BIRDS IN A BIRDBATH
with yellow daisies

In warm summer months birds can't resist a cool dip in a birdbath. With a tray of fresh water, you can attract a rainbow of species to your yard, such as red Northern Cardinals, blue Eastern Bluebirds, and yellow American Goldfinches. Keep your birdbath shallow so that even small birds can hop in for a splash. Placing small stones or twigs in the water can help birds maintain their footing while they drink.

BLOSSOM: There are about 4,000 species of daisies, which are found on all continents around the world, except Antarctica. They are actually "two flowers in one," their outer petals called "ray florets," and their small tubular flowers called "disk florets" inside. Its name is thought to come from Old English "daes eage," which means "day's eye," believed to have been named for the opening of their petals at dawn.

Birdbaths

Birds in a Birdbath

GRAY CATBIRD
and cosmos

Did you hear a *meow* coming from that pile of branches? It is a sneaky Gray Catbird, calling from its perch amidst brush and foliage. Creating a brush pile in your yard from tree and bush clippings is a wonderful way to provide a food-filled refuge for all sorts of creatures, especially cover-loving species such as catbirds.

BLOSSOM: You don't have to have a green thumb to grow cosmos. You pretty much just sprinkle the seeds in the ground, and they'll come up on their own. Pick a sunny location, thin seeds to just a few inches apart, and then wait for the beautiful pink and white blooms. They will last well into the fall and offer a good source of seed for birds.

Gray Catbird

GRAY CATBIRD

CALIFORNIA SCRUB-JAY
and California poppies

Jays are some of the smartest birds around. Not only do they cache a portion of their meals—saving them for later when times are tough—but they will try to make sure no other jays are watching as they hide their food. You can bring these beautiful blue birds to your yard by offering peanuts. See if you can find where one hides a peanut from your feeder!

BLOSSOM: California poppies are one of the most popular orange flowers for gardeners. While they grow as a perennial in warm climates, they can also multiply as an annual. Just sow the seeds like you would for sunflowers or cosmos, and then thin them to a few inches apart. They are naturally drought-tolerant, and easy to grow in any sunny garden space.

California Scrub-Jay

California
Scrub-Jay

URBAN BIRDS
with garden veggies

Green urban spaces can be havens for birds such as American Robins, which will thrive on invertebrates living in a rooftop garden. Project FeederWatch data show us that American Robins are becoming more common in winter, perhaps because places such as those urban gardens are so full of delicious snacks! Mourning Doves and House Sparrows will visit your garden for seeds, and Chimney Swifts will swoop overhead hunting for aerial insects.

VEGETABLES: Have you ever left veggies up in your garden and noticed the birds stopping by? It could happen. Veggies like lettuce can "bolt," which might lead to a bitter taste for you, but a great treat for the birds. Once the harvest in your veggie garden is done, let it keep growing. You just might attract some bird visitors that you didn't expect!

American Robin   Chimney Swift

URBAN BIRDS

FEEDER ALL-STARS
and cardinal flower

To bring an all-star cast of birds to your yard, offer a tube feeder with black-oil sunflower seeds. This oily seed is a favorite of nuthatches, titmice, finches, and woodpeckers, just to name a few. You might even see them all at the same time if your feeder is big enough, although sometimes the smaller species have to wait their turn and let the bigger species eat first.

BLOSSOM: Cardinal flower is popular among gardeners who don't have full sun in their yard because it still does well in shade. Also known as a hummingbird favorite because of the red blooms, cardinal flower is native to much of North America, and is a great addition to a native plant collection in your backyard.

Bird Feeder

Bird Food

Feeder All-Stars

CEDAR WAXWINGS
and mulberry

With their mischievous mask and porcelain-like plumage, Cedar Waxwings are a delight to have in your yard. You may notice them passing overhead in large flocks, giving high-pitched *seeee* calls. If you have berry-producing trees in your yard, then you may get to watch waxwings gluttonously feasting on the fruit.

BERRY: Most trees that provide berries for birds have fruit in fall or winter, but the mulberry is an exception. The fruit on these trees peaks in mid to late summer. Since the trees can grow to 50 feet, depending on species, this can make for a lot of berries. Some people might view mulberry as a messy tree because it produces so much fruit, but this is actually a good thing because there are enough berries for both you and the birds! The two species native to North America are the red mulberry (*Morus rubra*) and Texas mulberry (*Morus microphylla*).

Cedar Waxwing

Cedar Waxwings

RED-BELLIED WOODPECKERS
and joe-pye weed

Red-bellied Woodpeckers may have red heads, but they get their name from a wash of red that isn't always visible on their bellies. Data from Project FeederWatch show us that Red-bellied Woodpeckers are steadily expanding their range, so even if you don't have them in your yard now, you may soon. You can attract woodpeckers to your yard by leaving dead trees standing (trimming a bit, if necessary, so they don't pose a hazard). Woodpeckers will excavate holes for their nests, and insects feasting on the rotting tree wood will provide a key source of food for woodpeckers and other birds.

BLOSSOM: While "weed" is in its name, it's definitely not a weed. Joe-pye weed is a fantastic native plant that will thrive in backyard gardens. Hardy in zones 4 to 9, this plant with purplish-pink blooms can easily reach up to 6, 7, and even 10 feet tall. Butterflies love joe-pye weed.

Red-bellied Woodpecker

Red-bellied
Woodpeckers

COMMON GRACKLES
and sunflowers

In fall, huge numbers of blackbirds such as Common Grackles may descend upon feeders. They flock during the nonbreeding season, helping each other find food and evade predators. Despite their abundance, Project FeederWatch counts show us that Common Grackles are in decline. To provide a picturesque food source for blackbirds, let sunflowers go to seed in your garden and watch the resulting feast!

BLOSSOM: Sunflowers have plenty of appeal after their peak blooming time in summer. Dried sunflower heads are like a bird magnet! Birds will stop for the seeds well into fall. If you don't have sunflowers growing in your own yard, consider buying some in summer and drying the seedheads on your own. The birds will love this special treat when you put them out near the feeders.

Common Grackle

Common Grackles

EASTERN SCREECH-OWL
and maple tree

What species is easier to hear than to see? One answer is the Eastern Screech-Owl. Listen for their soft trills coming from the large trees in your yard at night. Screech-owls are common backyard birds, even though they can be hard to see. Those large trees in your yard may be home to more than you realize.

TREE: All maple trees are relatively fast-growing and display fantastic fall color, making them popular in backyards across America. If you live in the North and have dreams of tapping your maple tree for syrup, look for the sugar maple (*Acer saccharum*). Another good variety to grow in the East is the red maple (*Acer rubrum*). If you're in the South, look for the Florida maple (*Acer barbatum*). And, if you're in the West, look for Rocky Mountain maple (*Acer glabrum*). All are native to North America.

Eastern Screech-Owl

Eastern
Screech-Owl

DOWNY WOODPECKERS
and chrysanthemum

Downy Woodpecker pairs defend their territories year round, and if their territory encompasses your feeders, you will see the same birds again and again. Give your resident Downy Woodpeckers treats such as suet, a welcome source of energy.

BLOSSOM: It's important to offer nectar sources for birds, butterflies, and bees throughout the seasons. This is one of the biggest reasons mums are popular with gardeners. You can also have chrysanthemums in spring and summer, but they are especially welcome flowers in fall.

Downy Woodpecker

Downy Woodpeckers

AMERICAN CROWS
and sedum

American Crows may appear to be all black, but in the sunlight you can see subtle colors reflected in their glossy feathers. Crows are resourceful foragers that will take advantage of many sources of food, and they will help their family members by alerting them to delicious discoveries.

BLOSSOM: Since sedums have succulent leaves, they are one of the most drought-tolerant plants in the garden. 'Autumn Joy' sedum is one of the most popular with gardeners. It has beautiful green foliage throughout the season, and then it really steals the show in fall when the blooms are a rich pink color, which lasts all season.

American Crow

AMERICAN CROW

COMMON REDPOLLS
and juniper

Do you notice hundreds of tiny pinkish birds at your thistle feeders one year and none the following year? You might be witnessing the irruptive behavior of Common Redpolls. In winters when natural food sources are scarce, redpolls will visit your backyard feeders in hordes. They don't stick around because when natural foods become abundant again, they return to their more northern habitats.

BLOSSOM: Juniper is one of the most common shrubs in America because it adds color year-round, and you can plant it just about anywhere. While the blue berries of juniper might not be a bird's first choice to eat in fall, as winter hits, they become an important food source. Don't overlook this common, yet oh-so-important shrub for birds.

Common Redpolls

Common Redpolls

CAROLINA WREN
and blue spruce

In cold winters, the last type of bird you expect to see at your feeders is a dainty wren. But Carolina Wrens are showing up more and more at snow-covered feeders. Scientists have paired Project FeederWatch data with climate data, and think that mild winters may be allowing Carolina Wrens to expand their winter range north. If you offer peanut feeders or suet, you might find these wrens in your own backyard as they seek extra nourishment on cold winter days.

TREE: Often called the Colorado blue spruce, this evergreen is popular in the West, and it also has a beautiful blue tinge that makes it a popular Christmas tree. As a fairly fast-growing evergreen, it's an excellent choice for your backyard, especially if you want to provide cover for birds in winter.

Carolina Wren

Carolina Wren

BLACK-CAPPED CHICKADEES
with pine tree

Sunflower seeds are loved by chickadees: Black-capped Chickadees in the North and Carolina Chickadees in the South. For the holidays, you can offer seeds on a festive ornament. Spread some peanut butter between the scales of a pine cone and roll it in black-oil sunflower seeds. The oily seeds and fatty peanut butter are especially loved by birds in winter.

TREE: Pine trees are one of the best long-term investments you can make for your backyard. The pine cones can provide food for birds. The tree itself is a great place to nest. And, the year-round green of the tree's needles is a welcome bright spot in your backyard. Plant one or more, and you'll reap the benefits for years.

Black-capped Chickadee

Black-capped Chickadees

EVENING GROSBEAKS
with winterberry

What is that giant "goldfinch?" It is an Evening Grosbeak, a gorgeous yellow bird with an enormous bill for cracking seeds. Evening Grosbeaks will visit your feeders for seeds in winter, but they are visiting in fewer numbers now than in previous years. Data from Project FeederWatch show us that Evening Grosbeaks are in decline, but the reasons for this are unclear. By joining programs such as Project FeederWatch you can help identify species in decline so we can learn which most need our help.

BERRY: Technically part of the holly family, winterberry (*Ilex verticillata*) is native in most of the eastern United States. It grows up to 12 feet, though 5 or 6 is more common. As you might guess by the name, the bright red berries persist through winter, making them a popular (and much-needed) source of food for birds. If you need cover and food for your backyard, winterberry is a great addition.

Evening Grosbeak

Evening
Grosbeaks

PROJECT FEEDERWATCH

Project FeederWatch is a winter-long survey of birds that visit feeders at backyards, nature centers, community areas, and other locales in North America. Each year, 20,000 people count birds at their feeders for the project from November through early April, and send their counts to Project FeederWatch. With more than 1.5 million checklists submitted since 1987, FeederWatchers have contributed valuable data, enabling scientists to monitor changes in the distribution and abundance of birds.

Using FeederWatch data, scientists have studied the influence of nonnative species on native bird communities, examined the association between birds and habitats, and tracked unpredictable movements in winter bird populations. Join Project FeederWatch for the rewarding experience of watching birds at your feeders and contributing your observations to reveal larger patterns in bird populations across the continent.

HOW ARE FEEDERWATCH DATA USED?

The massive amounts of data collected by FeederWatchers across the continent help scientists understand:

- Long-term trends in bird distribution and abundance.
- The timing and extent of winter irruptions of winter finches and other species.
- Expansions or contractions in the winter ranges of feeder birds.
- The kinds of foods and environmental factors that attract birds.
- How disease is spread among birds that visit feeders.

 To learn more and participate, visit *FeederWatch.org* or use your Bird QR app and scan this symbol.

WATER SOURCES

Like all animals, birds need water to survive. Though they can extract some moisture from their food, most birds drink water every day. Birds also use water for bathing, to clean their feathers and remove parasites. After splashing around in a bath for a few minutes, a bird usually perches in a sunny spot and fluffs its feathers out to dry. Then, it carefully preens each feather, adding a protective coating of oil secreted by a gland at the base of its tail.

Because birds need water for drinking and bathing, they are attracted to water just as they are to feeders—a dependable supply of fresh, clean water is attractive to most birds. In fact, a birdbath will even bring birds to your yard that don't eat seeds and wouldn't visit your feeders. Providing water for birds can also improve the quality of your backyard bird habitat and provide you with a fantastic opportunity to observe bird behavior.

Birds seem to prefer baths that are at ground level, but ground level baths make birds more vulnerable to predators, and raised baths will attract birds as well. Change the water daily to keep it fresh and clean. You can also arrange a few branches or stones in the water so that birds can stand on them and drink without getting wet (this is particularly important in winter).

 To learn more about birdbaths, scan this symbol with Bird QR.

BIRD FOOD

SUNFLOWER

There are two kinds of sunflower—black oil and striped. The black oil seeds ("oilers") have very thin shells, easy for virtually all seed-eating birds to crack open, and the kernels within have a high fat content, extremely valuable for most winter birds. Striped sunflower seeds have a thicker shell, much harder for House Sparrows and blackbirds to crack open. Sunflower in the shell can be offered in a wide variety of feeders, including trays, tube feeders, hoppers, and acrylic window feeders.

WHITE PROSO MILLET

White millet is a favorite with ground-feeding birds including quails, native American sparrows, doves, towhees, juncos, and cardinals. Unfortunately, it's also a favorite with cowbirds and other blackbirds and House Sparrows, which are already subsidized by human activities and supported at unnaturally high population levels by current agricultural practices and habitat changes. Because white millet is so preferred by ground-feeding birds, scatter it on the ground or on low platform feeders with excellent drainage.

SHELLED AND CRACKED CORN

Corn is eaten by turkeys, cardinals, grosbeaks, crows, jays, doves, ducks, cranes, and other species. Unfortunately, corn has two serious problems. First, it's a favorite of House Sparrows, geese, bears, raccoons, and deer—none of which should be subsidized by us. Second, corn is the bird food most likely to be contaminated with aflatoxins, which are extremely toxic even at low levels. Never buy corn in plastic bags and never allow it to get wet. Corn should be offered in fairly small amounts at a time on tray feeders. Don't offer it in tube feeders that could harbor moisture.

SAFFLOWER

Safflower seed has a thick shell, hard for some birds to crack open, but is a favorite among cardinals. Some grosbeaks, chickadees, doves, and native sparrows also eat it. Cardinals and grosbeaks tend to prefer tray and hopper feeders, which makes these feeders a good choice for offering safflower.

NYJER OR THISTLE

Small finches including American Goldfinches, Lesser Goldfinches, Indigo Buntings, Pine Siskins, and Common Redpolls often devour these tiny, black, needlelike seeds. As invasive thistle plants became a recognized problem in North America, suppliers shifted to a daisy-like plant, known as *Guizotia abyssinica*, that produces a similar type of small, oily, rich seed. The plant is now known as niger or nyjer, and is imported from overseas.

PEANUTS

Peanuts are very popular with jays, crows, chickadees, titmice, woodpeckers, and many other species, but are also favored by squirrels, bears, raccoons, and other animals that should not be subsidized. Like corn, peanuts have a high likelihood of harboring aflatoxins, so must be kept dry and used up fairly quickly. Peanuts in the shell can be set out on platform feeders or right on a deck railing or window feeder as a special treat for jays.

MILO OR SORGHUM

Milo is a favorite with many western ground-feeding birds. On Cornell Lab of Ornithology seed preference tests, Steller's Jays, Curve-billed Thrashers, and Gambel's Quail preferred milo to sunflower. In another study, House Sparrows did not eat milo, but cowbirds did. Milo should be scattered on the ground or on low tray feeders.

MEALWORMS

Mealworms are the larvae of the mealworm beetle, *Tenebrio molitor*, and they provide a high-protein treat for many birds. Some people feed live mealworms to birds, while others prefer offering dried larvae. Birds such as chickadees, titmice, wrens, and nuthatches relish this food, and mealworms are one of the only food items that reliably attract bluebirds. Offer mealworms on a flat tray or in a specialized mealworm feeder.

SUGAR WATER OR NECTAR

To make nectar for hummingbirds, add one part sugar to four parts boiling water and stir. A slightly more diluted mixture can be used for orioles (one part sugar to six parts water). Allow the mixture to cool before filling the feeder. Store extra sugar water in the refrigerator for up to one week. Adding red food coloring is unnecessary and possibly harmful to birds—red portals on the feeder, or even a red ribbon tied on top, will attract the birds just as well.

GOLDEN MILLET, RED MILLET, FLAX, AND OTHERS

These seeds are often used as fillers in packaged birdseed mixes, but most birds shun them. Waste seed becomes a breeding ground for bacteria and fungi, contaminating fresh seed more quickly. Make sure to read the ingredients list on birdseed mixtures, avoiding those with these seeds. If a seed mix has a lot of small, red seeds, make sure they're milo or sorghum, not red millet.

FRUIT

Various fruits can prove quite attractive to many species of birds. Oranges cut in half often attract orioles, which sip the juice and eat the flesh of the orange. Grapes and raisins (no preservatives, please) are a favorite of many fruit-eating birds. Many species will also be attracted to the dried seeds of fruits such as pumpkins or apples. Be sure to dispose of any fruit that becomes moldy because some molds create toxins that are harmful to birds.

GRIT

To aid in grinding food, birds swallow small, hard materials such as sand, small pebbles, ground eggshells, and ground oyster shells. Oyster shells and eggshells are also a good source of calcium. If you decide to provide eggshells, be sure to sterilize them first. You can boil them for 10 minutes or heat them in an oven (20 minutes at 250 degrees). Let the eggshells cool, then crush them into pieces about the size of sunflower seeds. Offer the eggshells in a dish or low platform feeder.

To learn more about bird food, scan this symbol with Bird QR.

BIRD FEEDERS

GROUND

Many species of birds, including sparrows and doves, prefer to feed on large, flat surfaces, and may not visit any type of elevated feeder. Song Sparrows and many towhee species will readily eat fallen seed from the ground beneath your feeders. To attract these species, try spreading seed on the ground or on a large surface, like the top of a picnic table. You can also use ground feeders that sit low to the ground and have mesh screens for good drainage.

SMALL   LARGE

LARGE AND SMALL TUBE

A tube feeder is a hollow cylinder, often made of plastic, with multiple feeding ports and perches. Tube feeders keep seed fairly dry. Feeders with short perches accommodate small birds such as finches, but exclude larger birds such as grackles and jays. The size of the feeding ports varies as well, depending on the type of seed to be offered. Note that special (small) feeding ports are required for nyjer seed to prevent spillage.

LARGE AND SMALL HOPPER

A hopper feeder is a platform upon which walls and a roof are built, forming a "hopper" that protects seed against the weather. Large hoppers attract most species of feeder birds, and allow larger species, such as doves and grackles, to feed. Small hoppers attract smaller birds, while preventing larger species, such as grackles, from comfortably perching and monopolizing the feeder.

SUGAR WATER

Sugar-water feeders are specially made to dispense sugar water through small holes. Choose a feeder that is easy to take apart and clean, because the feeder should be washed or run through the dishwasher frequently.

PLATFORM

A platform feeder is any flat, raised surface onto which bird food is spread. The platform should have plenty of drainage holes to prevent water accumulation, and a platform with a roof will help keep seeds dry. Trays attract most species of feeder birds. Placed near the ground, they are likely to attract juncos, doves, and sparrows.

THISTLE SOCKS

Thistle "socks" are fine-mesh bags to which birds cling to extract the seeds. Seed within thistle socks can become quite wet with rain, so only use large ones during periods when you have enough finches to consume the contents in a few days.

SUET CAGE

Suet or suet mixes can be placed in a specially made cage, tied to trees or smeared into knotholes. Cages that are only open at the bottom tend to be starling-resistant but allow woodpeckers, nuthatches, and chickadees to feed by clinging upside down.

WINDOW FEEDERS

Small plastic feeders affixed to window glass with suction cups, and platform feeders hooked into window frames, attract finches, chickadees, titmice, and some sparrows. They afford us wonderful, close-up views of birds, and their placement makes them the safest of all feeder types for preventing window collisions.

To learn more about bird feeders, scan this symbol with Bird QR.

SOURCES

The primary source of information for this book was *The Birds of North America Online*, published by the Cornell Lab of Ornithology and American Ornithologists' Union at *bna.birds.cornell.edu*

Bonter, D. N., and M. G. Harvey 2008. Winter survey data reveal rangewide decline in Evening Grosbeak populations. The Condor 110(2): 376–381.

Chai, P., A. C. Chang, and R. Dudley 1998. Flight thermogenesis and energy conservation in hovering hummingbirds. Journal of Experimental Biology 201(7): 963–968.

Chiarati, E., D. Canestrari, M. Vila, R. Vera, and V. Baglione 2011. Nepotistic access to food resources in cooperatively breeding Carrion Crows. Behavioral Ecology and Sociobiology 65(9): 1791–1800.

Dally, J. M., N. J. Emery, and N. S. Clayton 2005. Cache protection strategies by Western Scrub-Jays, *Aphelocoma californica*: implications for social cognition. Animal Behaviour 70(6): 1251–1263.

Hamilton, Jr., W. J. 1943. Nesting of the Eastern Bluebird. The Auk 60(1): 91–94.

Meléndez-Ackerman, E., D. R. Campbell, and N. M. Waser 1997. Hummingbird behavior and mechanisms of selection on flower color in *Ipomopsis*. Ecology 78(8): 2532–2541.

Payne, R. B. 1981. Song learning and social interaction in Indigo Buntings. Animal Behaviour 29(3): 688–697.

Princé, K., and B. Zuckerberg 2015. Climate change in our backyards: the reshuffling of North America's winter bird communities. Global Change Biology 21(2): 572–585.

Rohwer, V. G., and J. S. Y. Law 2010. Geographic variation in nests of Yellow Warblers breeding in Churchill, Manitoba, and Elgin, Ontario. The Condor 112(3): 596–604.

Wolf, B. O., and C. Martinez Del Rio 2000. Use of saguaro fruit by White-winged Doves: isotopic evidence of a tight ecological association. Oecologia 124(4): 536–543.

Cover: American Goldfinch. Back Cover: Northern Cardinals. Page 3: White-winged Dove. Page 4: Verdins. Page 6: Red-bellied Woodpecker. Page 9: Rose-breasted Grosbeak. Page 82: Downy Woodpeckers. Page 83: Black-chinned Hummingbird. This page: Eastern Bluebird.